D1071018

Copyright © 1989 Victoria House Publishing Limited, Bath, England.
This edition first published in 1989 by Gallery Books,
an imprint of W.H. Smith Publishers, Inc.,
112 Madison Avenue, New York, New York 10016.
Reprinted in 1990.
Adapted by Andrew Langley.
Illustrated by Chris Rothero.
All rights reserved.
Printed in Great Britain.
ISBN 0-8317-8025-8

Gallery Books are available for bulk purchase
for sales promotions and premium use. For details,
write or telephone the Manager of Special Sales,
W.H. Smith Publishers, Inc., 112 Madison Avenue,
New York, New York 10016. (212) 532-600.

The Story of Christmas

Illustrated by Chris Rothero

Adapted by Andrew Langley

GALLERY BOOKS
An Imprint of W. H. Smith Publishers Inc.
112 Madison Avenue
New York City 10016

The road to Bethlehem was dusty, noisy, and crowded with hundreds of people on their way to the city. They were traveling to Bethlehem because the Roman Emperor had just made a new law. He commanded that everybody should return to the town where they were born so that he could count the number of people in his kingdom.

Among the crowd were Joseph and his wife, Mary. Joseph was worried about making the long journey to Bethlehem because Mary was expecting a baby very soon.

When they arrived in Bethlehem, it was growing dark and the streets were full of people. Mary and Joseph tried to find somewhere to stay. They went from inn to inn, but they found that all the rooms were full. Everywhere they went they heard the same answer: "I'm sorry, but we're very busy. There's no room at the inn."

At last a friendly innkeeper said they could stay the night in his stable. Joseph wished they could have a room at the inn. But Mary did not mind. She remembered the wonderful promise the angel Gabriel had made to her: "Your baby will be called the Son of God. He will be born a king and his kingdom will never end." Mary looked around at the oxen and the donkey. "The animals are gentle and kind," she said. 'God will be here with us."

That very night Mary's little baby boy was born. The ox and the donkey huddled close to keep them warm. Mary wrapped the baby in swaddling clothes and laid him in a manger filled with straw. "We shall call him Jesus," she said.

Not far from Bethlehem, there were some shepherds guarding their sheep from the dangers of the night. They had lit a fire on the hillside to keep warm.

All of a sudden, they saw a bright light up in the sky. There above them was an angel of the Lord, and the glory of God shone all around them. The shepherds were struck with fear and hid their faces. "Don't be afraid," the angel said, "I have wonderful news for you. It will bring great joy to everyone in the world. Tonight a baby has been born in the city of David, and he is the Son of God!"

At last the shepherds were brave enough to look up. The angel continued his message, "This is how you will find the child. He will be lying in a manger, wrapped in swaddling clothes."

All at once the whole sky was filled with angels, shining more brightly then ever before. The angels were singing their praises to God:

"Glory to God in the highest!
Let there be peace on Earth!
Let there be good will among all
the people of the world!"

As soon as the angels departed, the shepherds began to talk about what they had seen. "This news has come from God!" said one. "Let's go straight to Bethlehem," said another. "We must see the wonderful baby which the angel told us about."

The shepherds were so excited that they ran as fast as they could to Bethlehem. They carried with them the youngest lambs. When they reached the stable they saw the baby lying in the manger. Beside him sat Mary and Joseph, and around him the animals stood hushed and still. It was only a humble stable, yet the shepherds knew that they were looking at the Son of God. They fell to their knees and worshiped him, and offered the lambs as gifts to show their love.

The shepherds left the stable and went out into the streets. They told everyone they met about the wonderful sight they had just seen. The townspeople were amazed. God had long ago promised to send them a savior. Could this baby really be God's son? After the shepherds had spread the news they went back to their flocks, praising God and rejoicing.

Far away in the East, three wise men saw a new star in the sky. They looked in their books and found out what the star meant. It was a sign, promised by God long ago, to show that a new king had been born. The wise men decided to go and find the baby and worship him. They set out on a long journey across mountains and deserts, following the bright star.

At last the wise men reached Jerusalem. They went to King Herod and asked his priests where the newborn baby might be found. One priest said, "It was written long ago that a new king would be born in the town of Bethlehem."

The wise men were overjoyed when they heard this. They thanked the priests and set out again. The bright star went on in front of them. When they reached Bethlehem, the star stopped over the stable where Jesus lay sleeping. The wise men knew that they had found the child they were looking for. They got down from their camels and rushed into the stable.

The wise men saw Jesus lying in the manger with Mary watching over him. They knelt down and took out the gifts they had brought: gold, frankincense, and myrrh. One by one they laid the gifts in the straw at the baby's feet. Then they bowed their heads before the Son of God. Jesus opened his eyes and smiled.

As Jesus grew, he became strong and wise. He was a friend to all animals and all people. Mary smiled when she remembered the wonderful secret God had revealed to her. Her baby had been born to bring the love of God to the whole world.